Crazy Making

James Nugent

Introduction

I was a counselor in private practice for 22 years. It was only after I retired from service, that I began to really understand how much pain the family and friends of a mentally disordered persons may really suffer.

In the fall of 2014, a friend ended up being involuntary committed for a 2 week stay in a mental health treatment center. Since my friend's family knew that I had a background in mental health; they immediately enlisted my support and advice. I made it abundantly clear that I was no longer a practitioner but as a friend and fellow human being I could try to be supportive.

Disclaimer

The following short story is based on very true events. However, certain details have been changed in order to guarantee the privacy of every person involved. I feel that any identifying details will cause more harm than good. So out of respect for my friends; details were changed. There are many important things we all can learn from this story. For this I am grateful. This booklet is not psychological or legal advice. It is just a story.

Seek professional advice.

In the beginning

Two days after Tim's commitment; I and his sister Jan made a visit to the treatment center. I had rarely visited institutions like this and was actually quite curious. We were not allowed to bring: food, weapons, alcohol or valuables into the secured facility. Then we were asked to turn in our cell phones. I felt naked without my cell phone. The guard who turned out to be one of the therapists, gave us the "once over" with a metal detector. He told me to keep my reading glasses with me. I found out later that the lenses in the glasses could be broken and the used to kill an employee or commit suicide.

Apparently there is the possibility that visitors will try to smuggle dangerous objects or things that would facilitate an escape. I will talk more about Tim's attempts to escape later.

We were led through two locked doors and three long halls and then we sat down in a public room of sorts. There were couches and tables and plastic chairs. The patients were friendly and it was a pleasant in the visiting room.

Tim arrived and looked disheveled. Here was rapid in his speech and made no sense. We were alarmed but the therapist later explained that they were trying to figure out what were the correct dosages of several medications. It seemed reasonable so I volunteered some information to help.

Tim (my friend) had been lying to therapist for years. He often hallucinated all sorts of things and was often in fear for his life. In the past, I spoken to his therapists many times about these issues. Tim had a restricted list of who could have information about his mental health.

The law kept me from freely exchanging information with the therapists. While the Therapists were restricted in discussing Tim's treatment with me; there was nothing to keep me from providing information to the therapists. It was awkward but I gave them key pieces of information.

Sadly, the therapists changed often. I had to gain the trust of several therapists. I am more or less sure that it was noted that Tim was having hallucinations. I am also sure that nobody did anything about it. Tim lied and an overworked case managers/therapists dismissed it.

Be that as it may, Tim was at this time, stark raving mad and even he admitted that he needed a rest. We told Tim to rest and we promised to visit him in a few days.

The Second Visit

Two days later we visited Tim. He was generally rational but presented a wide variety his usual eccentricities. Actually since we were used to his eccentric behaviors; we were not good judges of his ability to manage his life. We stayed for an hour but something was really unsettling about our conversation. It took hours for both of us to calm down. I think we were both upset because we probably had been in denial about how mentally ill Tim has been for years.

The Third Visit

Tim was insane. He said that the doctor and Police and the court were in a conspiracy to keep him locked in. He said that he wanted to go a have a beer and perhaps go to Costco. He asked me to switch places with him. When I laughed because he and I look so differently; he said it wasn't funny. Then he scolded me even more.

He then began to fake cry and cling to his sister. He repeated nearly a hundred times that it wasn't fair and it was all a misunderstanding or illegal and a violation of his rights. He was dressed to leave and expected us to break him out. He was inconsolable when I explained that there was a locked door and a huge guard. Besides he needed to stay and get well.

Then Tim asked me if he could borrow my glasses. I said, "No." I also assure Tim that when it was safe he would get his glasses returned to him.

He swore and made a disturbance. He was the most disturbed and disturbing person in the whole place. I and Jan were drained after an hour of this. His crazy behavior made us feel crazy too.

We mistakenly promised to return in three days. We said we were both out of town until then. I felt this was a mistake for us to return so soon. But perhaps he would be better when his meds kicked in. I felt it was pointless to visit him in his present state. It just escalated his delusional thinking and behavior. Besides it was extremely emotionally painful for us to see him so psychotic. The more we cared, the more we were disturbed by what we saw.

We spoke briefly to his therapist and were told that Tim's behavior was wildly variable because of his bipolar state. This was a new diagnosis, and it fit Tim.

A few days later, I was over at Jan's house when Tim called. He sounded really nonsensical. So we decide not to visit him yet. Tim got it in his head that he was going to get out of the facility the next day. Jan told him that once he was better, he would get out.

I also suggested that the doctors might require that a professional visit his home a few times a week to make sure he was taking his meds and managing his life. He didn't like that.

The Fourth Meeting

We visited Tim and he seemed better. However, Tim was an expert at faking wellness and so I doubted that he was ready to go home. The doctors and therapists were not so sure either.

Jan and I were asked to go to a release review board hearing the next day. When I asked why, they said that with Tim's condition, somebody would have to agree to help support Tim in the community and be a contact? He would need a formal support network and plan.

I said that I would not be doing that and that Jan would have to think about it. If Tim was not ready to live alone, he would have to be released to a group home or be sent to the State Mental Hospital. We were told that there was a waiting list at the mental hospital. I said, that perhaps a group home was their only choice. Jan was distraught.

There is something inside family and friends that wants mental illness in our loved ones to go away. There is a natural tendency to minimize and ignore bizarre behavior because we desperately want things to go back to the way they were. Then is occurred to me and Jan that Tim has not been well for years.

The hearing was not the next day or the day after that. It was decided that Tim was not even close to being ready to go home. Strangely, Tim also failed to ask anybody about his release date; mostly because he would have to behave well until the date.

Tim can be a bully when he doesn't get what he wants from you. A decade ago he wanted a ride to a bar from me. He wasn't supposed to drink while on his medications. I gently reminded him of this. He then proceeded to call 11 of my relatives and friends who each dutifully called me and told me to be nice to Tim! I was not going to give in to the coercion.

Those people who could understand that Tim was using them to inflict revenge got my new phone number. Five friends and relatives who just didn't get it, never did get my number again.

I tried to preserve the relationships by asking that they never talk to me about Tim. I noticed that those who were so easily manipulated by Tim; did eventually cut off all contact with Tim over the years.

It was peaceful at my house for a long time. Slowly Tim got back into my life. A few years after I cut off direct communication with him, he was occasionally in my social network. He generally did not try to bully me and was very careful about exposing his antisocial behaviors around me.

Somehow local businesses (owners and managers) started discreetly reporting Tim's abusive and disruptive behaviors to me. For example, when Tim imagined wild dogs in a restaurant and threw water everywhere; the manager contacted me and the police. I said I would talk to the therapist. The store banned him from the property.

Over the years the incidents had grown in number and severity. I could not get help for Tim because he kept lying about his mental state to the mental health professionals.

At least the police over the years were wise in how they managed Tim. Although they had to threaten to Taser him more than once.

The day Tim was committed, he was found in the backyard of the house where he was renting the basement. He had spent the night in the yard face down in his boxer shorts. Somebody reported a dead body. When the police arrived they didn't know what to do. Tim got a warm blanket and a ride to the hospital. Later he was transferred to the mental health facility. He didn't remember any of it.

The effect on his family was devastating. Many of his siblings stayed out of it. His elderly mother ignored his birthday. Tim worked some relatives with the phone privileges he was aloud. Several of his relative stopped answering their phones. Those who dared care, were in anguish because of Tim's constant manipulations.

Tim left me a phone message. He was complimentary and calm. He wanted me to find a free lawyer to work to spring him from the mental health facility. I ignored the call. Tim needed to get help and was fouling up his treatment by lying about his symptoms.

There were several manipulations where he attempted to leave the facility. One comically ridiculous attempt backfired badly. A week or so after his commitment, he said that his mother was taking him out of the facility. When one relative repeated the story to another; all hell broke loose. The story got changed to the claim that his mother had indeed just walked him out of the facility.

The facility would not disclose to family if Tim had escaped or not. They were generally not on Tim's list of people with whom information could be shared. Nobody thought to call Jan because they didn't know she was on the list.

Multiple calls were made to Tim's mother who was taking a break from all the chaos caused by Tim. She was not answering the phone for the evening. Family members collaborated and called the police. Police were dispatched to Momma's house to retrieve Tim. The poor elderly widow was shocked and angered when she ended up talking to police officers in the middle of the night. Everybody whom was made a fool, stopped talking to Tim. Tim remained in involuntary commitment.

The next day I got to be at ground zero too! Tim called me and said that he was finally getting out. He told me to take off work and come get him. Then he wanted to go get a beer and then pick up his cat from a friend. I said I had not heard from the discharge nurse that this was going to happen and that I wouldn't be taking time off from work to help him escape. He ignored my protests. He was adamant about what about what I was going to do. I gently told him that he still needed a little time for the doctor to get his drug dosages correct and that it will be all ok in a week. He was not accepting "no" for an answer.

Tim said he also wanted me to find a free lawyer. He wanted to sue the doctor. I also said "no" to that and told Tim not to call me tomorrow. I didn't want to hear from him.

The next day Tim called my cell phone intermittently throughout the day. I did not answer. He also spent the day calling other people who then left messages about disappointed they were in me. I seriously considered getting a new number again. It's free to change. After all these years couldn't these people figure out that they are being used as a tool to enable antisocial behavior? I decided that I didn't want to be in a 45-minute conversation with each person.

So I left a long winded message on my voice mail. Basically it said that if you want to maintain a relationship with me, do not leave me any messages about Tim. He is not well at this time and the doctors are adjusting his meds. There were 5 messages all wishing me a restful night and or a good day tomorrow. I almost cried from their kindness.

After the fiasco with the police, Jan and I decided to not visit or talk with Tim for a while. When Tim was eventually released he would have to take a bus or taxi across town.

Some professional cleaning had happened to his apartment in his absence. Tim would need to take care of some things. There was a blood stain on the living room rug and fire burn on a wood floor. There was a cracked window and hand prints on the ceiling. It would be therapeutic and healthy for Tim to be forced to clean up a little of his own mess. He would of course try to get somebody else to do it. However, most people who knew Tim would not be fooled into dealing with the cleanup.

Personal Responsibility

Tim's shirking of personal responsibility was legendary. His mantra was "I'm mentally ill so I am not responsible." Anything he didn't want to do; fell under this mantra. Playing helpless was his lifestyle. Tim considered part time work or volunteer position out of the question. If anyone even suggested that it would be good for him volunteer a few hours a week; Tim would marshal a legion of people who "cared" in order to punish the offender. Some of the caring people would actually threaten the victim on behalf of Tim.

I experienced the wrath of Tim a number of times over the years. My offenses where usually gentle suggestions that Tim could take some small personal responsibility in his life. For example, I thoughtlessly suggested that Tim could cook a few meals at home and save some money. The consequences to me were disruption to my social life and family relations for weeks.

In my opinion Tim is allowed to be such a problem because he is bullies everyone. Nobody wants to stand up to him. At one time he was extracting hundreds of dollars a month out of his family so that he could wander the community and eat three meals a day out.

Everyone knew (even Tim) that it was costing $600 a month, when he could make his own meals at home cheaply. Be that at it may, Tim would have his way and somebody else would have to pay the cost. They would pay in emotional abuse or money.

The Discharge Nurse calls me.

Margaret the Discharge nurse left a message. She said the 4 days hence Tim would be discharged and she was having difficulty getting anybody to pick him up. She asked me to do it.

I declined to answer her message. I just didn't want to get involved anymore. Tim had stressed me out. I wasn't sleeping well and having trouble concentrating and it was all because of Tim's manipulations and bully tactics.

Tim leaves a message.

Tim called and ordered me to pick him up and gave me a list bills and chores the he wanted me to address. I could answer the message and disappoint him or avoid the conflict. I chose to not be abused. I chose to not return Tim's call.

Released and Free to Pillage

With no open beds at the state mental hospitable, Tim was eventually released. He was back in action again.

Unwelcome in several restaurants; he would continue to make scenes and coerce money out of other establishments. His favorite trick was to claim that cashier at a store had short changed him. Often if the manager didn't know him, they gave him the money in order to stop the loud disruption.

Another trick he often used was to start crying and claim he lost his $2 bus money. Eventually a kind hearted person would give him the money. Off he would go to the next victim.

Some of the schemes were brilliant. He hit up local churches for several thousand dollars of aid even though he was already well funded. Then, he would also get financial support from family and friends. He had more cash on hand than I ever had. When I told him that it was dishonest to scam this money; he said he was saving for a rainy day in the future.

Anybody who doesn't say and do what he wants is called mean. He said I was mean.

Making sense of crazy making

I think that Tim is mentally ill and a bully and a petty criminal. Until somebody holds him accountable for his schemes and bully behavior; he will continue his disturbed and disturbing life. As long as Tim lies about his symptoms he will relapse and be involuntarily committed again. As for me I am staying as far away as possible from Tim. I will do this even if it means that I give up my network of friends. The price of staying in the disturbed network is too high.

Epilog

Tim has a visitor from the mental health people, who tries to keep track of Tim's medications. Funny thing, even if the pill count is correct; there is no way to know for sure if he is actually taking the drugs.

I spotted Tim in the mall the other day. He was trying to shake down the ice cream vendor but had forgotten he had already done his routine to this establishment in the past. The manager called the police. Tim was screaming, "you can't touch me, I am mentally ill."

As the cops closed in, I walked the other way. I hoped the cops didn't get hurt. I hoped that Tim didn't get hurt.

Maybe I should have watched and used my cell phone to record the interaction. Then again, I would just get sucked back into the disturbed and disturbing world of this very unusual mental patient.

Best Regards

James Nugent

12-5-15

Books by James Nugent

Living on the Edge of Civilization

How I Sailed from Olympia to the San Juan Islands, and Returned Safely

An Alternative Boating Guide to Southern Puget Sound

Twenty Hours under the Sea

Without Speech

Miracles in Young Cove

Home Self-defense

How and Why I lived Aboard

Kayaking Budd Inlet in South Puget Sound

Writing E-books and Making the Perfect Book

I Speak Esperanto

The Rainbow Road and Other Signs of God's Love

Write a Book

Living an Abundant Life, Within Your Means

Crazy Making

Social Jujitsu and Powerful Principles for Managing Social Conflict

Advanced Social Jujitsu

Blackjack on My Small Budget

A Little Benedictine Oblate Manuel

Without Speech

All things work

Loving Time with Your Creator

Personal Adventures in a Life of Learning

Loving Time with Your Creator

The Good News about Being Catholic

The Extraordinary Eucharistic Visitor

E-book Writing and Overcoming Barriers to Creativity

Living an Abundant Life Within Your Means

E-book Writing and Organizing Your Ideas

Paddling to the Rhythm of God

My Forty Days for Life 2013

Lifestyle Reality Observing

How to Sail in the Winter

How to Get Your Kid to Move Out

How to Get What Want

Sex, Abstinence, and Happiness

Cynthia Says Radio Show – Anger is a choice

Eight Things You Need to Survive

Three Moms from Hell

Moving and Starting Fresh

More Good News about Being Catholic

The Solo Kayak

Everyday Survival Kit

Rainy Day Kayak

Night Kayak

Solo Kayak II

Paddles and Water

A Beach Naturalist on Southern Puget Sound

Clean House Clean Life

The Total Catholic Christian

Advanced Social Jujitsu

The Beginning School Counselor

Managing the Most Difficult Students

Not Taking Responsibility

Happiness is a Choice

Why Write?

The Voyages of Saint Bernadett

Available at Amazon.com in Kindle E-Book and or Audible Book or Paperback

www.ingramcontent.com/pod-product-compliance
Lightning Source LLC
Chambersburg PA
CBHW060107300526
45787CB00018B/1857